The Journey to Self-Forgiveness

Rhonda Word Rushing, PMHNP

ISBN:9798479160059

DEDICATION

Dedicated to Lane

In memory of my mom

CONTENTS

ACKNOWLEDGMENTS

I would like to acknowledge my husband for always supporting me in my pursuits. My dad, Robert Bellew, for encouraging me to go to college and my mom for always believing in me. I also want to acknowledge my babies who taught me about loving unconditionally. I thank God for the amazing gifts he has given me. And lastly, D. Davis for her tutelage and mentorship.

"The weak can never forgive. Forgiveness is the attribute of the strong."

Gandhi

1 INTRODUCTION

Forgiveness is an age-old concept. It is a core view of many religions and philosophies. In the Jewish faith, forgiveness requires repentance. Christianity promotes unconditional forgiveness. Islam encourages followers to convert grief into a compassionate act. Mental health and social sciences expound on the benefits of forgiveness for the forgiver. For as long as humans have made mistakes, forgiveness has been of great concern.

Forgiveness of oneself is a bit different. Self-forgiveness is an opportunity to engage in self-examination that results in changes for the better. It is not an act witnessed by others, but, rather, an arduous inner-journey toward accepting responsibility, healing self-esteem, and improving mental health. Just as each act requiring forgiveness is different, each person will have a different path toward personal growth and insight. This enlightenment occurs when we acknowledge, learn, and grow.

By logical deduction, for inner emotional turmoil to have resulted from a mistake, a strong sense of right and wrong must be present. There is an assumed proportional relationship between morality and emotional distress resulting from our actions. In other words, requiring forgiveness of self is a strong indicator of innate goodness. Learning to forgive ourselves of past indiscretions requires the courage to examine our culpability for those behaviors. This can be unpleasant and discomforting. By accepting responsibility for our actions, we begin to see the world beyond our own vantage point. and how our actions and behaviors affect mankind.

"Every struggle in your life has shaped you into the person you are today. Be thankful for the hard times, they only make you stronger."

Keanu Reeves

2 WHAT IS THERE TO FORGIVE?

Since the Garden of Eden, mistakes exist and will continue to be a plague on the morality of man. Acts that require forgiveness, particularly self-forgiveness, abound with many negative emotions. Two of the most damaging of these emotions are guilt and shame. These feelings lead to loss of self-esteem, poor self-worth, self-doubt, and self-loathing. Negative emotions, like these, create chaos in our emotional core. If the core, or soul, of a human being is imagined as an empty cylinder, it can hold negative or positive emotions.

Acts that require forgiveness are typically associated with pain, anger, hatred, shame, remorse, etc. When these emotions are held inside the core, it does not leave room for positive emotions like peace, happiness, and love. Learning to release the negativity is the challenge of self-forgiveness. Acts which cause real or perceived harm can be damaging to oneself or others. It is possible that some acts harm only the perpetrator. These acts are damaging because they go against the moral grain of the individual. When this happens, it can be more the person's perception of the act than the act itself. The perception of the wrongdoing is based on each individual's personal beliefs. Individuals raised with a strong sense of right and wrong can be more likely to develop anxiety and inner turmoil over acts they perceive as innately wrong. From a philosophical view, it requires goodness to feel shame and guilt.

Emotional turmoil results from perceived wrong-doing. Acknowledging responsibility for our actions often causes humiliation, regret, shame, and remorse. These are powerful emotions and are difficult to reconcile. Feeling ashamed relates to whatever activity is causing strife. Individuals may misconstrue the hatred of the act for hatred of self. Self-loathing can damage the ability to interact with others and destroy self-worth. This cyclic thinking of being morally bad, undeserving of forgiveness, and, therefore, undeserving of love can lead to multiple mental health disorders. Creating negative views of self becomes part of the inner monologue we have in our mind. Feelings of remorse and humiliation may hinder the ability to move past the incident. Two big steps toward self-forgiveness are accepting responsibility and understanding the context of emotions. To judge behaviors from the past based on who we are today is not logical. Without a compassionate understanding of damaging events, people in this ethical dilemma can become stuck. It is akin to an emotional carousel with the same events replaying again and again. This type of thinking never gets beyond the initial event. The cliché of forgiveness being a journey requires visualizing a direct path. It requires acknowledging an end goal of understanding oneself. With the goal in sight, it is easier to convert the circuitous path into a direct path toward understanding.

All lessons require moving from one point to another. Think of a child learning to read. Without conquering the lesson at hand and moving forward in their endeavor, they will read at a kindergarten level forever. It is the same concept with reconciling past acts. This process requires taking steps toward the end goal. There is an old saying about the way to eat an elephant is one bite at a time. Tackle overwhelming tasks one step at a time.

Why is forgiveness so highly rated? As discussed, many negative emotions link acts or behaviors that warrant forgiveness. Long-term exposure to toxic emotions creates increased risk of mood disorders, like depression and anxiety. It can also cause stomach distress, heart disease, high blood pressure, and increased risk of death. With prolonged exposure to the stress and anxiety generated by these emotions, the body stays in a constant state of fight or flight. The body is perpetually on stand-by for a possible tragic event. Forgiveness is a means of reconciling these emotions and making them manageable. Forgiveness neither excuses our behavior nor decreases the validity of the person's concern. It does put the event into a reasonable context. This act enables learning and healing to occur.

When iron ore is taken from the ground, it requires blending, firing, beating, and shaping before it is recognizable as anything of value. The end product is hardened steel. The experiences that help us grow and develop are similar to the brutal process of forming steel. We are who we are because of the lessons learned. Just remember, some of those lessons can be brutal!

"The simple truth is we all make mistakes and we all need forgiveness."

Desmond Tutu

3 MAKING MISTAKES

Human beings make mistakes. That is a universal truth. Since mistakes can vary greatly, the effects of mistakes also vary. It would make sense that the result of the mistake would be in a positive correlation with the mistake itself. For example, accidentally hitting a beloved family pet with your car would generate more remorse than unintentionally backing over the neighbors' trash can. Although any scenario can have extenuating circumstances, the concept is similar to the punishment should fit the crime. This train of thought requires examination of the mistake within the context of the circumstances. For this writing, we will examine errors of internal conflict, morality failures, and self-injurious thinking.

Mistakes should be examined within the scope of the act. It is logical that the more severe the act, the harder to find forgiveness. The severity of the act is affected by the perception of the perpetrator. This process is another step in the reconciliation of our behavior. Examination of the offensive behavior is necessary. One key part of the examination is: Was anyone harmed? Was the act illegal? How do I make restitution? Acts involving others are a different type of forgiveness and beyond the scope of this writing.

Some of the circumstances affecting our behavior can be:

Timing.   Teen years are rife with mistakes. Peer pressure, the influence of the internet, and raging hormones can have drastic effects on behaviors. Mistakes made in adolescence are the result of an immature brain. The prefrontal cortex is responsible for impulse control and understanding long-term consequences. This part of the brain does not mature until the late twenties. Cognitive development lags behind physical development during adolescence. Thought processes are not fully formed. Additionally, not all teens mature at the same rate. During these years, it is essentially an adult body with a childish mind.

Severity of the Offense. For the sake of this writing, we will assume that there was either no harm to others or reparations with the injured party have been completed. Now it comes to examination of the harm it has done to self. Why was the behavior appealing in the first place? What has happened in the past that draws us to this behavior? Was there truly awareness of the consequences of behavior at the time? The idea of self-forgiveness is not an opportunity to make the behavior acceptable, but it is a critical time for understanding our inner-self. Ignoring these issues creates a festering wound that will not go away. Just like a physical wound that has become infected will not heal itself, neither will an emotional wound. The physical wound will become septic, depleting the body's natural defenses, and eventually, cause death. The emotional wound will also continue to grow and deplete the mind's ability to manage the problem. Approach this opportunity as a surgeon; dissect it, cleanse it, and let it heal.

Black or White. Life is like a movie in Techni-color. There are no limitations to the variations of colorful emotions we can produce in our lives. Imagine trying to reduce the world down to simply black or white. There are many shades in between black and white as evidenced by some of the most amazing photography ever made. The award-winning works of Ansel Adams in black and white photography are astounding. All the intricacies and subtle nuances of color captured on black and white film are anything but simply black or white. There are times when right and wrong can be the same. Extenuating circumstances play a big part in the perception of 'wrongness' seen in any situation.

Victimization. A significant influence on behavior is a history of victimization. Abused individuals often carry guilt and feel ashamed for the abuse they suffered at the hands of another. Children frequently feel responsible for the mistreatment and abuse they endure. Abuse in childhood often creates emotional distress requiring professional help. These emotional wounds alter the forming thought processes in a young person's brain. While a history of abuse does not guarantee a future of deviant behavior, it does affect how we see the world and ourselves. It significantly contributes to the negative inner monologue that can replay in our minds.

Consider an abused child. As children, our universe is formed by the adults in our lives. The child's mind does not know or understand that the abusive behavior they are experiencing is not normal. Until the child is exposed to a more normative environment, they do not understand their victimization. Many children suffer severe emotional wounds. These children cannot fathom that the world will not always be the way it is currently. As the brain matures, these damaging experiences have become internalized into their forming thought processes. Often these victims feel they have done wrong and the abuse was their fault. Nothing can be further from the truth. Problems develop when these thoughts become hard-wired into our permanent thinking. Emotional wounds are the hardest to understand. They are not visible to others but they create tremendous self-doubt and pain for the victim.

Internet culture. Many adolescents spend a lot of time online playing games, watching anime, and living in an online culture. Internet gaming and online reality are linked to the same pleasure circuitry in the brain as gambling. The addictive properties of this online lifestyle create difficulty when youth are transitioning to the real world. This culture is also linked to increased pornographic exposure through animation, video game graphics, and sexualized themes. These internet activities result in dopaminergic activity in the prefrontal cortex which is not fully matured. Prolonged exposure to these activities become habit forming.

Exposure to these online cultures at an early age can create emotional confusion for the immature brain. There is a sense of safety when our reality is lived almost exclusively online. To the immature brain, there is limited culpability for online activities. As the brain matures and we view these activities as questionable, it can create emotional upheaval. This, again, goes back to the timing of the event. When the brain is emotionally immature and exposure to these activities begin at an early age, it is impossible to understand the extent of damage due to online behavior. We must also consider how the under-aged individual was exposed to questionable online graphics and animation. Was the exposure to sexually explicit animation part of the abuse process? This requires further exploration in the theory of victimization.

Dysfunctional families. As stated earlier, children are completely at the mercy of the adults in their life. Family dysfunction can result in difficulty for children developing coping skills and mastering their surroundings. Dysfunction can result from many sources, like broken homes, substance abuse, combined families, extreme poverty, mental illness, and physical debility, just to name a few. These situations result in children assuming a role in the family that facilitates their survival. This maladaptive pattern of behavior becomes part of the developing psyche.

As part of the brain's amazing survival instinct, it will develop alternative methods of function to promote survival. For example, after a person has a stroke, the brain will form off-shoots of blood vessels near the area of damage so a blood supply to that part of the brain can be re-established. This is called collateral circulation and it is a method of preserving brain function. Emotional trauma is very similar.

Our brain forms behavioral mechanisms to help us cope with emotional wounds. An example would be a child growing up with an explosive, alcoholic parent. This child may learn submissive behavior to avoid the wrath of the parent. This pattern of behavior carries over into adulthood. Whenever an emotionally stressful situation occurs, these adults may retreat to their familiar path of submission and withdrawal. They are often fearful, anxious, and feel responsible.

Growing up in a dysfunctional family causes children to take on multiple roles within the family. As a result of the dysfunction, children have problems with boundaries, poor ability to resolve conflict, and poor self-esteem. They often assume a caretaker role. These families may cause a blurring of roles and responsibilities that creates confusion for the immature brain.

Coping Mechanisms. As adults, it is more difficult that we realize to form health coping mechanisms. We learn from our environment how to interact and react with others. Unhealthy coping mechanisms are often a result of our childhood influences. We may get angry and act our aggressively when our feelings are hurt instead of finding a way to talk calmly to the other person.

Addiction. Expounding on the theory of the dysfunctional family, it is easy to see how a child that grows up with an alcoholic parent learns that the way adults deal with stress is to have a drink. They learn behaviors as well. Perhaps dad has drank too much to drive to the store to buy more cigarettes. Mom is busy with household chores and puts off going to the store for him. When dad 'throws a fit' mom drops what she is doing and goes gets cigarettes to keep the peace. Dad is then happy because he got what he wanted. Mom has been manipulated into becoming an enabler. The child growing up will typically either learn that they want nothing to do with alcohol or if they throw a big enough fit they will get what they want. These children learn by watching interactions in their environment to expect immediate gratification, at any cost.

Children of parents with addiction often grow up facing the same dilemmas as their parents and turn to the same coping mechanisms. Many patients who are in Alcoholics Anonymous must address the people they have wronged. Behaviors resulting from addiction are ones that are influenced by circumstances. People change when they are no longer under the influence of chemicals. Realize the behaviors were committed by a different person than who you are now.

4 THE SELF-CRITIC

Guilt is an emotional response focused more on what effect our behavior has on others. Or, just as damaging, what effect our behavior will have on how others view us. Feeling guilty and ashamed creates a weight that grows with time. The self-critic feeds on these emotions. Imagine an obnoxious imp following us everywhere we go. His job is to reinforce all the negative inner monologue going through our mind. Now, think about someone with a weight problem. The imp is at every function saying, "Go ahead, fatso, have a cupcake. That's why your clothes don't fit. You are a fat loser and nobody likes you and you will never amount to anything." Or, "See there, chunky, they are all watching to see if you go back to the buffet ... again."

We know this is not true. This is distorted thinking. Logic dictates that having a cupcake does not make anyone a loser. Having a weight problem does not mean you are unliked and unloved. Nobody is watching you to see if you go back to a buffet because they are eating their own meal. This interplay is an example of how the self-critic internalizes every situation to think the worst of self. These thoughts are part of a long-term inner-monologue. Whether the thoughts are placed there by our own beliefs or by the negative things told to us during childhood, they are ingrained in our thought processes.

Negative inner monologues are not uncommon. This demeaning interchange feeds negative self-esteem. It is easier than one may think to internalize the turmoil resulting from mistakes into the belief that we are bad. This is also distorted thinking. This replay of insulting thoughts is formed by the neuroplasticity of memory responses. This process is a combination of psychological and brain-based responses to our environment. Altered cognitive processes that produce these negative responses are also linked to depression. It is easier to resort to the automatic thoughts than to stop and think about things logically. When a situation occurs creating stress and anxiety, we panic. The brain will take the path of least resistance. It will choose the well-worn path of negativity. Working to replace these thoughts with positive, realistic thoughts works in the same repetitive manner.

Our thought responses, whether logical or not, are formed via the process of neuroplasticity. The brain is triggered to respond through events in the environment. The repetitive thoughts triggered by external events become like rote memory and automatically occur. Internalized negative thoughts are an example of how children who are told they are dumb, ugly, fat, bad, etc. have difficulty believing otherwise. The children often grow up believing they are not worthy of good outcomes, not as good as others, and undeserving of forgiveness. These thoughts go along, unchallenged, for years and last well into adulthood. Imaging the crushing weight of self-deprecating rhetoric these people have heaped upon themselves through the years.

Psychological addiction and coping mechanisms work on the same principal. Perhaps a former drinker discovers their spouse is having an affair. The stressful thoughts trigger the automatic response to want to drink because this was their coping mechanism in the past. Then, the distorted negative thinking occurs. "I had a drink. I am a loser, no wonder my spouse found someone else."" I don't deserve to be loved."

The inner critic is the most difficult critic to overcome. We are not bad people; we are good people who may make bad choices. Everyone deserves forgiveness and peace. Change the way you view things. Apply logic to every   situation.

5 LIFE LESSONS

In business, errors and mistakes are analyzed with a root cause analysis [RCA]. The purpose of an RCA is not to dole out punishment for the offender, but to fully analyze and understand what happened to cause the error. This allows management to gain insight into the root of the problem. Policies and procedures are reviewed, diagnostics are performed, and staff training is developed to prevent the same mistakes from occurring in the future. The process of self-forgiveness is similar to an RCA on humans. It is dissecting and analyzing errors so that the appropriate reconciliation can be made. Life lessons are usually difficult, painful, and heart-rending; otherwise, they would not be of much value. If lessons are not learned, the same mistakes are likely to continue. Just like a baby learns not to touch the heater when they burn their hand, adults get an equally painful, but different type of burn. Individuals typically learn from acts resulting in unpleasant sensations.

When considering life lessons, unpleasant emotions serve a purpose. It acts as a form of moral self-correction. Unlike a child that may get swatted on the hand for errors, adults have only their inner core, or soul, to provide correction and guidance. We can consider the relationship of morality and emotional distress. The more upset we are over our behavior, the higher our moral expectations. Human beings are motile and in a constant state of change; both physically and emotionally. From birth, interactions with other people and the environment shape and form the developing individual. Just like water takes the shape of the container, humans are also shaped by the environment around them. Part of the environmental interaction for people includes making mistakes. Individuals, like organizations, would never learn without making mistakes. Training and teaching modules are developed by individuals who tried, failed, learned, tried again, and succeeded. Without a mistake, there is no lesson; without a lesson, there is random chaos.

Along with emotional motility in humans, there is also resilience. Like the water in the container, once the water leaves that container it flows onward and is no longer bound by the constraints of that environment. For individuals struggling with constraints of emotional turmoil, forgiveness is the way to remove these boundaries. Removing our negative emotions requires work. There are many cognitive behavioral techniques used to assist people in working through these situations. Using worksheets, journals, role play, and many other therapeutic activities help to let go of emotional trauma. Individuals learn by removing the restrictions of emotional upheaval.

If we consider addictive behavior, we see altered function as a result of the addiction. It does not matter what the addiction is to, addiction is the need for repeated behavior that is self-damaging. Whether addicted to substances, alcohol, or negative thinking, rehabilitation often requires multiple attempts to change. These changes require a re-learning of lifestyle, thought processes, and life choices. A thorough examination of self and the results of our behavior, similar to the RCA, is required. This is one of the necessary steps, not only to recovery, but to healing. As a society, we have learned to view addiction as an illness. Addiction to unhealthy thought processes can be viewed as the same.

The best things in life often result from making change. The benefit is often not seen right away which can cause stress and anxiety, even fear. It is easier to stay in a bad situation than to face the uncertainty of modification. Even though a situation is unhealthy, we know what to expect from it. Our expectations are set to what we know can be expected; thereby, lowering our chances of disappointment. When faced with change, individuals can become overwhelmed with the unknown. We must learn to view change as what it is: opportunities to grow!

6 FORGIVENESS

Forgiveness entails tremendous inner strength. It is an act of allowing our soul to be free of negative feelings and emotions. This requires acknowledgment, inspection, and resolution of our inner turmoil. The concept of forgiveness may sound simple but there are some complex ideologies that coincide with forgiveness. When others have caused us pain and suffering, it is easier for some to forgive others than to forgive self. Forgiveness allows freedom from the harmful emotions that have filled the inner core. The only way to fill the core with peace is to get rid of emotional chaos. This process requires understanding the act in the appropriate context, exploring the emotions caused by the act, and attempting to negotiate these emotions. We must accept who we are, despite our faults, and believe we have a unique existence and a purpose in the universe.

One concept that demonstrates the effect acts have on our emotional health is to imagine that every hurtful act is on a rock. Just as the events that have occurred are different in size, the rocks that represent them are different sizes. Throughout life, events deal out demeaning and damaging rocks. If the rocks are carried around with us, it will not take long to be overwhelmed by their oppressive weight. Each person has the choice to either drag the negative emotions that the rocks represent around, or put the rocks into their proper context. Forgiveness is the way to give the rocks back and become free of the burden.

Removing the burden of guilt and shame gives our soul freedom. It takes time and work, but freedom from negativity and pain can be accomplished. Thoughts of failing to be a good person or bringing shame to family members are difficult to overcome. It is often easier to forgive a friend, or even a stranger, than to forgive oneself. One possible explanation is that individuals may exaggerate the severity of the act or the negative consequences of what happened. Objectivity is often diminished because the offending party is self.   As discussed earlier, the perception of wrongdoing is relevant to our beliefs. Sometimes, individuals are their worst enemy and their own worst critic. The impact of the occurrence is dependent upon our moral perception. The terms of right and wrong may have gray areas for some while others see the world in strictly black or white.

When we have a history that results in negative thought processes, self-doubt, and poor self-esteem, we form maladaptive coping mechanisms. Negative thoughts become who we believe we are. If a child is told they are dumb and unable to do anything correctly, they believe this to be true. These words become seeds of doubt that form thoughts deeply rooted in our psyche. These negative thoughts can become our comfort zone. It is easier to believe the imp when he tells us we are a loser than to challenge those illogical beliefs. The child who was told they were dumb by their parents will struggle to find the confidence to try. As discussed earlier, when faced with stressful situations, some people panic. The automatic thoughts we live with are the first thoughts in our mind during emotional challenge. Each negative thought, toxic emotion, and damaging memory can weave itself, thread by thread, into our very own security blanket. It is easier to accept the negative we are familiar with than to challenge this way of thinking and change our view. Knowledge is the best tool for self-empowerment.

Find the strength and courage to forgive yourself.

7 HEALING

Universal Truth: Let it Go

The Gospel of Mark is referring to the belief in God that can make all things possible through faith. Belief in a higher power is imperative when searching for the meaning of life events. Many belief systems are founded in love and forgiveness. The belief in being deserving of forgiveness and being worthy of love are also key in learning to heal. Individuals must have determination to improve. Often, a situation does not get better in one or two attempts to change. Healing the soul takes time and requires a legitimate attempt to relearn negative thinking. Internal wounds associated with negative thinking can be just as deadly as major physical trauma. Self-healing requires empathy. Many people can find empathy for others but find it difficult to find empathy for themselves. Mistakes are inevitable, but learning prevents the mistakes from being a constant source of pain. If not been properly packaged and put away, the negative emotions in our core continue to erode the self-esteem.

Faith. Faith helps us face each day through the belief that God loves us and He wants the best for us. Psalms 65:3 tells us that although we are overwhelmed by our sins, God forgives us. Christianity teaches us that God has created us and knows everything about us from our cellular function to the number of hairs on our head. If we believe this, we understand that God did not create a mistake. When Jesus chose his disciples, he chose them as they were, faults and all. God views us the same. Faith does not promise that it will make life easy, but is does promise possibility. Our

15

search for meaning in life is made easier with faith. Teshuva is the act of atonement, part of the process of forgiveness in the Jewish faith. The Qu'ran 42:40 tells us that God rewards those who pardon and remain righteous. In Islam, there is no peace without forgiveness. Find your path to inner peace.

Journaling. Through journaling, thoughts and emotions are symbolically removed from the core and put on paper. Journals also chronicle the progress of changing perspective. Keeping records of thoughts, emotions, and improvements allows introspection and growth. As the path to healing evolves, a journal creates a sort of map to revisit in times of strife. It allows further healing and it creates a means of helping others.

Keep a private journal of the progression to forgiveness.
What are the emotions evoked?
How are the emotions managed?
What was learned as a coping skill?
How have the journal entries changed?
How have thought processes changed?

Perform an RCA. The perspective of the incident and ensuing emotions should be re-evaluated. Look at the mistakes from an analytical point of view. Most notably, was a lesson learned and was a change in behavior initiated? This RCA of the incident will provide an algorithm of preventive action.

What was the root cause of the problem?
Was a life lesson learned from the incident?
What was the cost of the lesson?
What impact did the action have on others?
How can the error be avoided in the future?

Motility. As discussed, humans are always changing. The mistakes made in life create the lessons that are learned. When the toxic emotional environment is freed from its core, the wisdom of healing occurs. In the analogy of emotions being like water, they flow within the constraints of their boundaries. Individuals have the power to alter the flow of emotions through managing emotional responses.

Create a road map of events that have left a lasting impression. At every fork in the road there is a decision made. While a poor decision leads to a negative event, there is a positive decision to change. Re-visit your path of errors and positive changes.

How did the event effect the road taken?
How will the knowledge learned change your path?
What are the positive changes you have made?

Essence of Self. A valuable lesson to take away is that each individual is more than just one mistake. Think about perfume. It is a combination of flowers, weeds, grass, animal excrement, coal tar, and other things that are not pleasant if taken on individual merit. When the items are combined and distilled down, they become a lovely fragrance. Humans are the same. If individual aspects of success, failure, sadness, happiness, love, hate, etc., are examined, they are not impressive. But when they combine, they form a wonderfully unique individual defined by so much more than one mistake. The simple fact that you are reading this book means you are stronger than you think. You have more courage than you believe and more potential than you ever dreamt possible!

Consider positive attributes, past successes, significant friendships, and unique traits that distinguish individuals one from another. As if making a perfume, list the ingredients of your unique individual.

What would be the marketing slogan?

What would the scent be called?

Who would the product appeal to?

Self-Respect. Take stock in accomplishments. Self-respect is highly linked to morality and wisdom. It takes a strong moral character to acknowledge wrongdoing. Without the strength of character to see wrong in our actions, there would be no emotional fallout. As discussed, the activities requiring forgiveness are rife with toxic emotions. If the emotional dilemma was not significant, there would be no problem. It can be postulated that the purpose of negative emotions is to guide morality. By that same token, if an individual is inundated with the negative emotions of shame and guilt, that is an indication of being a morally sound person.

It both requires and develops wisdom to learn from mistakes. When the causative behavior is removed, this indicates a lesson learned. When the repercussions of behavior are severe, lasting lessons are learned. Learning that past events are permanent but the response to the events is controllable requires wisdom. Learning that the individual has the choice of how to respond to circumstances, either caused by others or by self, also develops self-respect.

Be Creative. Use art or music as a form of expression. Many famous artists, like Edvard Munch and Vincent Van Gogh, used painting as a way to deal with pain. Music is a powerful emotional outlet. Writing is a wonderful tool for creative expression. Creativity can be a great way to release negative emotions and turn them into a thing of beauty. Being creative does not require artistic ability, just the desire to create. Find what intrigues you and pursue it.

Find your Role. One tremendous part of coming full-circle with healing is helping others. We know that everyone makes mistakes. So, by that logic, we can assume that many others are also struggling with their own self-forgiveness. Through empathy born of experience, we can help guide others to their own form of healing. Utilizing our lessons helps other individuals see that healing is possible. We also serve as proof that wounds heal, with time, and we learn through our pain.

If you have completed these steps, you have everything you need to start turning your tragedy into your life's work. There is none better to heal a wounded bird than another wounded bird. The wounded bird has empathy and compassion. They understand the struggle and are prepared to really listen. Make a difference in the world by sharing your story.

"When we are no longer able to change a situation — we are challenged to change ourselves. "

Viktor Frankl

8 CONCLUSION

Mistakes are a universal truth and are part of everyone's past. Time cannot be reversed, deeds cannot be undone, and facts cannot be altered. What can change is our perception of the past. Learning to forgive is tantamount to self-awareness and growth. Through acknowledgment of mistakes, valuable lessons of morality and responsibility are learned. It is not possible to accomplish peace without learning through the pain. Lessons are painful, that is why they leave a lasting impression. Self-adjustment and improved self-awareness lead to the empowerment of knowledge. Arm yourself with the awareness of who you are and the knowledge needed to make good choices. If we do not take an active role in changing the world, the world will change us. Take the bad you have experienced and put something good back into the world. Help others who are struggling and learn how fulfilling it can be to view the world outside the scope of self.

My path that brought me to this point was painful. I have suffered emotional abuse from childhood through adulthood. I was bullied in school. My childhood was filled with humiliation and rejection. I used to think God had forgotten me. I felt like an extra in everyone else's life because I did not have children. With time, I was blessed with a nephew and niece that are like my own children and now with 3 'grandsons' that I love and adore. I have an amazing husband.

With the encouragement of my dad, I went to college and got my first degree at age 34. I then returned and graduated with a nursing degree at age 50. After losing my mom to dementia, I wanted to do more; to give back. I started the path to graduate school. I was working full-time and studying in the Doctorate of Nursing Practice program at the University of South Alabama. In December, 2019, while exactly half-way through graduate school, I had a stroke. I then had two more strokes that week. The last stroke of the series was devastating. While driving me the 2-hours to the hospital, I asked my brother to have my church pray for me. I was also praying! I believed it was not a question of if I was going to die, but when. Another of God's blessings in my life is that I got out of the hospital on December 23, 2019.

At the suggestions of family and the support of my wonderful husband, I quit working but I continued school. Right after the strokes, I had difficulty finding my words and I was mentally fatigued very quickly. I found a new way of learning that worked for me and I graduated with a Master's of Science in Nursing in December, 2020, at the age of 58. God has continued his blessings! I passed my national certification exam on my mom's birthday, January 26, 2021. I know she was smiling!

Victor Frankl is one of my favorite theorists. He survived Auschwitz and went on to write some amazing philosophical theories on man's search for a purpose in life. My favorite of his views is on the ability of the mind to control the power we allow others to have over our emotional well-being. We cannot make the bullies be nice people but we can work to take the sting out of their words and deeds.

If there is a message here, it is that just because someone says something negative about you does not make it true. I was told I wasn't smart enough to go to college. I was told I was too overweight to be pretty and men don't marry fat women. You do not have the power to change the behavior of others, but you do have the ability to remove their power over you. You are not at fault. You deserve love, happiness, and peace. You are beautiful because you are what God has created. It is ok to be different and, most importantly, you are stronger than you realize.

Forgive yourself, accept God's blessings, and become the healed bird that helps other birds learn to heal.

Bibliography

Al Ubaidi, B. A. (2017). The cost of growing up in dysfunctional family. *Journal of Family Medicine and Disease Prevention, 3*(3), 3:059. Doi.org/10.23937/2469-5793/1510059.

Biography.com Editors (2017, October 1). 15 inspiring Gandhi quotes. Retrieved from https://www.biography.com/news/gandhi-quotes.

Bradberry, T., & Greaves, J. (2009). *Emotional intelligence 2.0.* San Diego: Talent Smart.

Cardinal, Catherine. (b. 1953). *AZ Quotes.* Retrieved from https://www.azquotes.com/quote/839530.

Dalai Lama. (b. 1935). *Brainy Quote.* Retrieved from https://www.brainyquote.com/authors/dalai-lama-quotes.

Elliott, J. E., & Elliott, K. (2000). *Disarming your inner critic.* Lafayette, Louisiana: Anthetics Institute Press.

Enright, Robert D. (2001). *Forgiveness is a choice.* American Psychological Association.

Frankl, Viktor, E. (1962). *Man's search for meaning: An introduction to logotherapy.* Boston: Beacon Press.

Hall, Julie H., & Fincham, Frank D. (2005). Self-forgiveness: The stepchild of forgiveness research. *Journal of Social and Clinical Psychology, 24*(5), 621-637. Doi:10.1521/jscp.2005.24.5.621.

Hill, Jr., T. E. (1991). *Autonomy and self-respect.* New York: Cambridge University Press

Joyce, James. (1882 - 1941). *Brainy Quotes.* Retrieved from https://www.brainyquote.com/authors/james-joyce-quotes.

Kaslow, F. W. (Ed.). (1996). *Handbook of relational diagnosis and dysfunctional family patterns.* John Wiley & Sons.

Lewis, H. B. (1971). *Shame and guilt in neurosis.* New York: International

Universities Press.

Lichtenfeld, S., Maier, M. A., Buechner, V. L., & Capo, M. F. (2019). The influence of decisional and emotional forgiveness on attributions. *Frontiers in Psychology, 25*, https://doi.org/10.3389/fpsyg.2019.01425

Nietzsche, F. (1973). *Beyond good and evil.* Middlesex, England: Penguin Books.

North, J. (1987). Wrongdoing and Forgiveness. *Philosophy, 62*, 499-508. doi:10.1017/S003181910003905X.

North J. (1998). The "ideal" of forgiveness: A philosopher's exploration. In In R. D. Enright & J. North (Eds.), *Exploring forgiveness* (1st ed. pp. 15-34). University of Wisconsin Press.

Peterson, S. J., Van Tongeren, D. R., Womack, S. D., Hook, J. N., Davis, D. E., & Griffin, B. J. (2016). The benefits of self-forgiveness on mental health: Evidence from correlational and experimental research. *The Journal of Positive Psychology 12*(2), 159-168. https://doi.org/10.1080/17439760.2016.1163407.

Pierro, A., Pica, G., Giannini, A., Higgins, E.T., & Kruglanski, A.W. (2018). "Letting myself go forward past wrongs": How regulatory modes affect self-forgiveness. *PLoS ONE, 13*(3), e0193357. https://doi.org/10.1371/journal.pone.0193357.

Price, R. B., & Duman, R. (2010). Neuroplasticity in cognitive and psychological mechanisms of depression: An integrative model. *Molecular Psychiatry, 25*(3): 530–543. doi: 10.1038/s41380-019-0615-x

Rangcanadhan, A. R., & Todorov, N. (2010). Personality and self-forgiveness: The roles of shame, guilt, empathy, and conciliatory behavior. *Journal of Social and Clinical Psychology, 29*(1), 1 -22.

Smedes, Lewis B. (1996). *The art of forgiving: When you need to forgive and don't know how.* New York: Random House.

The New Jerusalem Bible. General editor, Henry Wansbrough, Doubleday, 1985

The Qu'ran. 42:40.

Tutu, D. (1998). Without forgiveness there is no future. In R. D. Enright & J. North (Eds.), *Exploring forgiveness* (1st ed. p. xiii). University of Wisconsin Press.

Sadock, B. J., Sadock, V. A., & Ruiz, P. (2015). *Kaplan & Sadocks synopsis of psychiatry: Behavioral sciences, clinical psychiatry*. Philadelphia: Lippincott Williams & Wilkins

Yandell, K. (1998). The metaphysics and morality of forgiveness. In R. D. Enright & J. North (Eds.), *Exploring forgiveness* (1st ed. pp. 35-45). University of Wisconsin Press.

Zagefka, H., Jones, J., Cagler, A., Girish, R, & Matos, C. (2020). Family roles, family dysfunction, and depressive symptoms. *The Family Journal, 3,* 346-353. https://doi.org/10.1177/1066480720973418

ABOUT THE AUTHOR

Rhonda Rushing is a Psychiatric Mental Health Nurse Practitioner. She began her career in health care as an Occupational Therapy Assistant in 1997. She later returned to school to pursue a career in nursing. Throughout both career paths, her primary patient population was in psychiatry. Rhonda currently works in private practice and at an addiction and recovery Intensive Outpatient Program.